10 Life Lessons on How to Find Your Why NOW & Achieve Ultimate Success

John Di Lemme

10 Life Lessons on How to Find Your Why NOW and Achieve Ultimate Success

Di Lemme Development Group, Inc.
931 Village Boulevard
Suite 905-366
West Palm Beach, Florida 33409-1939
877-277-3339
www.ChampionsLiveFree.com

This book is designed to provide competent and reliable information regarding the subject matters covered. However, it is sold with the understanding that the author is not engaged in rendering legal, financial, or other professional advice. Laws and practices often vary from state to state and if legal or other expert assistance is required, the services of a professional should be sought. The author specifically disclaims any liability that is incurred from the use and/or application of the contents of this book.

ISBN: 978-0-557-01414-9

Dedication

My success is attributed to some very important people in my life. My parents, Philip and Mary Ann Di Lemme, raised me to be an honorable man and never take the easy way out. My grandfather, Philip Di Lemme, Sr., taught me the value of earning an honest income and that integrity is the foundation for a successful business. My brother, Mark Di Lemme, passed away at an early age and never had the chance to find his Why. My thoughts of him keep me focused on changing the lives of others and refusing to fail. My wife, Christie Di Lemme, is my rock and her unrelenting support reminds me daily that I am not alone in my quest to change the world. Her mother, Debbie Johnson, gave me her most precious gift, her daughter, and I am forever thankful. Without these people in my life, I would not be here today, and it is my honor to dedicate this book to them.

John Paul Di Lemme

Contents

Foreword
Fritz Musser

Often I ask someone the question, "What could you do if you knew you could not fail?" Greatness lies within all people. The key is unlocking and releasing that greatness from within.

I have known John Di Lemme for many years and have personally witnessed his passion and drive for life and success. He is relentless in pursuing his Why. You can believe that what he says will come to pass, because he never says it unless he believes it and he never gives up once he's says it. It's the power of your own words, and you can speak life or death with your words. John's words of life always come to fruition.

This book is a must for all to read. It doesn't matter where you are on the success ladder. You can be at the lowest point of your life or the highest point. Everybody has room for growth and improvement.

This book leads you strategically through the process of discovering your Why and cementing it into the fabric of your daily routine to personally experience what you once thought was difficult or impossible. John sees everyone as potential champions. He even says, "Champions make decisions and decisions make champions." You are a champion, and you have been given a certificate for life to become the best that you can be.

Now is the time for you to consume the powerful principles of this book, start your Why Card and get ready for the greatest season of your life. Your best days are ahead of you, and this book will place the tools in your life to accomplish greatness.

Catch the spirit of this book and what John Di Lemme has masterfully laid out for you. Read every page thoroughly. Do what he says and follow his advice. It will change your life forever. It is time for you to fly to greater levels of success and life. Enjoy the journey!

Introduction

At the age of eighteen, I was diagnosed as a stutterer and labeled by society as handicapped.   Little did I know that my stuttering would turn out to be a precious gift in my life. This so-called handicap became the driving force behind me creating the #1 most powerful success key in life...the development of a personal "Why."

Your Why is the reason that you do what you do everyday. From the moment you wake up, your personal guidance system that embodies your Why takes over. Your Why creates your

> I was looking to make a run for real change and became desperate to release the success maniac inside of me.

attitude for the day that allows you to face life's challenges, overcome obstacles and successfully complete all of the goals that you have set for that day and beyond.

Your Why is your purpose for living. It identifies (and then guides you toward) your ultimate goal in life. At the tender age of eighteen, I had no clue about my Why in life or what I wanted to do with the rest of my life.

At the time, I was working around the clock at my family's art gallery. I worked there, because it was low-risk, easy, and convenient.

Over time, I became tired of just going through life and not actually living it. So, like many of you, I became a looker. I was like a man in jail looking for a chance to escape. I was looking to make a run for real change and became desperate to release the success maniac inside of me.

Most successful people that I've met became desperate lookers at some critical point in their lives. Their desire to want something more out of life leads to their success. Are you a looker? If so, you may have the same problem that I encountered in my looking. I truly knew what I wanted, but I didn't have the vehicle (*the means of transportation*) to accomplish it. Over the last several years, I have seen so many people set goals and work very hard but never achieve them. Are you one of those people? The reason that you don't achieve your goals is because you are missing the vehicle, which is the driving force that will ultimately transport you to your desired results.

I am blessed to deliver my messages to audiences around the globe and meet thousands of wonderful people but I've noticed something that deeply disturbs me every time that I speak. Many of the event attendees continually go from seminars to conferences to conventions investing thousands of dollars in personal development materials yet NEVER achieve the results that they desire in their lives. It breaks my heart to see good people striving to reach their goals and dreams but end up failing time and time again. Why does this happen? These champions simply don't have the vehicle to get them to where they want to go in life.

Now, I ask you to be totally honest with yourself. Have you ever been in a situation where you seemed to have a life-changing breakthrough, but you eventually just fell back in the same, unchanged, unproductive habits? Didn't it frustrate you to invest your precious time and your hard-earned money without getting the results that you desired? I've got good news for you! It can be so easy to achieve what you desire deep in your heart, and you can do it without wasting anymore of your time and your money. This is the vehicle that I've been referring to that will catapult you to success.

The secret that I will share in this book is not known by the general public. They don't know it, because we live in a fast paced, microwave society that suffers information overload. We want everything quick and easy in which we end up skimming over new information – even information that can save our life! It's like a rock skipping across a pond that eventually sinks without ever reaching its destination.

This powerful magic force that you are about to unlock will only work for you when you give it some time to release all of its explosive power.

What I have to share with you has made thousands worldwide wake up and rethink their lives. Decide today to make an appointment with yourself and this book. Don't laugh. We all need to treat ourselves with as much respect as we treat others with whom we make appointments. This is your life that we're talking about! Have enough respect for yourself and your future to schedule quality time – with no cell phones, email or other distractions – in order to carve out a brand new life and path to success.

This powerful magic force that you are about to unlock will only work for you when you give it some time to release all of its explosive power. Time is the most valuable currency we have. That's right. Nothing else in all of life has the value of time. You must be willing to invest time in your quest from where you are now to a life full of abundance. Do you truly want to live your dreams and achieve your goals? This is a question that only you can answer. If your answer is "yes", then read this book. But, only when you have made an appointment with yourself and your destiny!

Lesson 1
The Most Important Day of Your Life

As life goes on day by day, we all experience challenging days and some really magnificent days, but there's one day in particular that is more important than any other day of your life. The most important day of your life is your birthday.

Why? At birth, we all start out the same. We are all on equal playing ground. Yes, I know we're all born into different external circumstances, but your birth certificate gives you the right to grow up and become a Champion. Your birth certificate is your Certificate of Life. Unlike a college degree, you automatically earn your Certificate of Life when you exit the womb. No questions asked . . . you are destined for success.

Sounds easy, but that's where most people fall through the cracks. Even equipped with this wonderful certificate that gives them the right to achieve miracles and become a Champion, many fail to do so. Why? They simply don't take the action that makes their success possible. Let me give you an example. It's like someone that has been given a million dollar trust at birth, but they never write the check to unlock the funds. Now, does that make sense? No, but neither does having a Certificate of Life that enables you to create miracles and then you simply choose not to use it. You and only you are ultimately responsible for your level of success or failure in life.

Your mind and your heart are like a parachute. There's only one way that they work – they must be open! An open mind and an open heart will allow the dream inside of you that develops throughout your life to become a reality. Your birth certificate *(aka your Certificate of Life)* gives you the right to achieve your dreams. From the moment of your birth, you are destined for massive success, monumental prosperity and an incredible amount of unbelievable results in your life. But, you control the chances of when or how or if that will happen.

Once again, every single person has the same starting point in life. It's guaranteed! It's not a 60-day, 90-day, 120-day or even a 60,000 mile guarantee. It is a lifetime guarantee! You are guaranteed at birth that you have the same ability to achieve success as everyone else. Your race, your gender and/or your physical handicaps don't matter. It's simply your decision of whether or not you achieve this success. Remember, Champions make decisions and decisions make Champions.

You are Not a Victim!

Let me explain what I mean here. We live in an age of victimization. We've been trained to think and live as victims.

> You are guaranteed at birth that you have the same ability to achieve success as everyone else.

Our whole culture is saturated with messages that "you cannot achieve because . . ." Some see themselves as victims of ethnicity, gender, being born into a low-income family, vast conspiracies, etc. If you regularly watch the evening news or brainwash yourself with other forms of negative, popular culture, then that victim mentality will become ingrained in your mind. That's why I advise people to avoid those messages and watch movies like "Cinderella Man" that reinforce the positive aspects of life and make you believe that you can achieve success despite the challenges that you face.

Victimization is a lie! Notice how victimization always relates to people as groups, but you and I are individuals. We are not groups! That's how the lie gets instilled. When you see yourself as part of a group (racial, economic, social, religious, etc.), then you begin to see your destiny as something that is out of your own hands. You jump on the bandwagon of failure, because you think that your future is already written according to the lives of others. That kind of deception keeps people from taking responsibility for and ownership of their own destiny.

Just Do It!

You are an individual created by God and given a wide open path to success. Take your birth certificate as a Certificate of Life that gives you as an individual the permission and the right to be successful.

Now, stand up and say out loud, "I am a certified champion by birthright. My certificate of life gives me the right to achieve success." Say it again, but this time say it with true conviction. Say it with power and genuine belief that you know it is true! You must believe before you can achieve. Go ahead. Say it over and over and over until you do believe that you can achieve massive results in your life.

When Jesus was in his earthly ministry, he often told people to do outrageous things. For example, he told his disciples to catch a fish and cut it open in order to find the money to pay taxes. Another time, he told them to go borrow a donkey. He also instructed a blind man to go wash in a particular pool of water to regain his sight. Would you say those are outrageous actions? Why did he do those things? Because he knew that when people actually do outrageous things, they unlock a dimension of power with themselves that they didn't even know existed.

This kind of power created by taking action blows the doors off the prison of passivity. Taking bold action is explosive power! It will often take us from a "do nothing" realm onto the higher ground of action, engagement and success. That's the reason that I often ask people to take specific action steps. As long as we just merely think, feel or believe, we remain passive. There's no action in thinking, feeling and believing. Have you

I like the old Nike advertising line: "Just Do It." Trust me. There is a great and priceless value associated with just doing it.

ever been in a situation when you really want to do something that you know will change your life, but you think "Oh, that would be silly to do that. I'm not going to embarrass myself. What would people think of me?" As long as you let those types of feelings and beliefs control your ability to act on something, you will remain in a prison of doubt and fear. But when you take action and do something that you know will make a difference in your life, a new realm of power begins to work inside of you.

Throughout the journey of this book, I will ask you to take action steps like standing up, speaking words out loud and writing down specific exercises. I like the old Nike advertising line: "Just do it." Trust me. There is a great and priceless value associated with just doing it without over-thinking it.

WARNING: I will challenge you to get out of your comfort zone, and this will make you uncomfortable at times. But no matter what, you must commit to completing all exercises and get beyond passivity and embarrassment. Once you learn to do that, nothing will be able to stop you from taking the action needed to achieve your dreams in life.

Once more, I want you to say out loud, "I am committed to my success!" Do you believe that? Say it over and over and over until you DO believe it. If you cannot do that, then you will not succeed. Don't go any further in your reading until you have made this commitment to yourself!

Time to Use Your "Certificate of Life"

Now, I'm going to ask you to do something else. Go get a copy of your birth certificate, laminate it and put it on your desk (or the dashboard of your car, the cockpit of your plane or any other work site). I like to call your work area "the construction zone." Why? Because you are going to BUILD your future there!

We will even develop blueprints along the journey that will lead to your future success. It's like building a skyscraper. There is a starting point for the visionary architect. He must know the purpose, style, height and other dimensions of the building and what supplies will be needed in the construction. Well guess what? Your birth certificate is your starting point. So, let's take action and begin building your future. You will look at your birth certificate everyday and remember that you are an individual not a group and that you have the right to be successful in every area of your life.

Decision plus action equals results. We need to recreate the daily process that creates your results. Every day is a phenomenal day. That's why it's called the present. You must treat everyday like a present, and open it with great expectation. Live each day as if it's a precious gift, because it is! Don't proceed any further with your reading until you have your Certificate of Life in front of you so that you see it every day. It serves as a reminder that you can and will achieve monumental success.

Re-Program Your Life!

Now that you have your Certificate of Life in front of you, I want you to look at it and say, "It's all my fault." That's right. Your life is your fault – good or bad. I can almost hear the chorus of readers now: "What do you mean, John? Why would you tell me that it's all my fault?" Okay, okay, it's actually your default.

Let me explain. As many of you know, I have a New York accent. I have a New York accent, because I grew up around New Yorkers. From the date of your birth until approximately the age of seven, your default in life is developed. Yes, it's a little confusing at first so let me explain further.

When you purchase a computer, it comes with certain programs that give it the ability to function when you turn it on. After you boot up, you choose new software, your internet provider and other technical features in order to make it suitable for you. But unless you successfully install and save your new software, your computer will always revert back to those original default settings. That is, unless you make a decision to change those defaults by saving your new programs.

By the age of seven, your mental computer has all of its defaults developed and installed on your hard drive. Think about that. How many times were you told as a young child, "Stop. Don't do that. Don't touch that. Don't talk to strangers. Stay away from them. Don't look at that. Don't, don't, don't, don't?"

> Your default setting creates doubt instead of hope for a successful future. So, when it comes to a decisive stage in your life and you step out in faith, you must understand that you are challenging your default.

You are told don't, do not, and stop about 17 million times versus the word "yes." This default is not only installed by your parents as a young child, but also your grandparents, relatives, babysitters, teachers, friends and anyone else that you may have spent time with growing up.

Your default setting creates doubt instead of hope for a successful future. So when it comes to a decisive stage in your life and you step out in faith, you must understand that you are challenging your default. How do you change this? Just like you make changes to a computer so that it's more suitable for your individual purposes, you must "install and save" new mental software in order to change your old default settings.

How do you do this? Eastern cultures understand the power of the spoken word much more than Americans do. When we speak words, those words take on a life of their own. Just as negative words spoken by others when we were younger have deep power in our lives so do positive words. A major part of installing our own software is found in the beautiful and magical mystery of speaking positive, life-affirming, future-positive words.

Simply speak affirmations that empower you to believe in yourself and the achievement of your goals, dreams and desires. You have the right to success, and you will succeed in the game of life! You must switch your default from "no, no, no" to "yes, yes, yes." This is not easy, because you are unlearning behaviors that have been on your hard drive since the day you were born.

If you are forty years old, then that's four decades of negative defaults that you must reprogram! It's not easy to do. It doesn't happen overnight, and it usually doesn't happen by reading one book. You must invest in personal success habits on a daily basis that break through those defaults that were cemented in your childhood.

I along with most educators believe that you must read or listen to something at least seven times before you truly grasp the concepts of the material. Why? Because we are a society of multi-taskers. This means that we often do several things at one time; therefore, we don't pay enough attention to any one thing and often miss the importance of what we are reading or listening to.

I suggest that you invest in seven different colored highlighters prior to reading this book. The first time that you read it, grab one highlighter and highlight what jumps out at you. Then, use a different color each time that you read it. I think you will be surprised by how much you missed the last time! You will also see that you internalize the reading differently on the 2nd, 3rd, 4th and successive readings because of the growth in your life.

Before our journey continues, we are going to begin recreating your defaults. Remember, this is a constant battle, and many people give up. Your default settings are very strong so you need to be even stronger in re-programming your life. Let's get started.

I want you to commit right now to doing this exercise every time you are led to fall back into your negative defaults. You must say out loud, "I am a Champion by birthright, and I will not let my negative defaults control my successful future." Will you do this?

Make a commitment right now to yourself by writing that affirmation below:

_____

_____

_____

_____

_____

Say it one more time just to get you comfortable with resetting your defaults. "I am a Champion by birthright, and I will not let my negative defaults control my successful future!"

Kick the Chicken!

Your negative defaults also known as "the past" will control your future only if YOU let them. The past tends to bind shackles around your ankles that hold you down as you try to proceed on your success journey. Close your eyes and imagine five hundred pound chains around each of your ankles as your pursuing your dream. It's impossible! You and only you can make the decision to rip the chains of your past *(your default settings)* off your ankles and start walking free from what has been holding you down all these years.

> You, and only you, can make the decision to rip the chains of your past *(your default settings)* off your ankles and start walking free from what has been holding you down all these years.

Many years ago, a minister gave a great illustration of this truth. He said that when farmers take chickens to the market, they will often tie their ankles and lay them in the bed of their truck for the ride to the sale barn. This prevents them from flying out of the truck.

When they arrive at the sale barn, he will take them out of the truck, place them on the ground, and then cut the cords, releasing them to get up. But, the chickens won't get up! They think they're still bound at their ankles so they just lay there. The farmer has to actually kick them so they flutter and finally get up. He went on to say that we must "kick the chicken" in ourselves in order to get out of our incapacities. So, kick the chicken in yourself. Your ankles are free!

As you go forward, don't use your past to determine your future. Do not make excuses based on your past. Burn the bridge to your past mistakes and limitations. Remember: If the bridge to your past is burned behind you, then you have no choice but to travel the path into a successful future. Develop your Why in life and begin to achieve things in life that you've only dreamed about. Remember, choosing success over failure is your decision.

Lesson 2
The Power of Commitment

Few things in life have as much power as *commitment*. Commitment turns average or inactive people into what the military calls a full metal jacket *(a bullet that can penetrate great obstacles)*. The character trait of commitment does that. It gives our dream the full metal jacket that it needs in order to punch through obstacles. In fact, I would say that commitment is the foundation for building your life. It is the bedrock of achieving your ultimate Why in life.

Let me ask you a question. Are you truly committed to achieving your dreams and goals in life? I'm sure you said "Yes." OK, let me ask you an easier question. Have you invested in the seven highlighters that I recommended in the last lesson?

If you haven't made the commitment to complete the exercises in Lesson One of this book, then stop right now, go back and do it. You cannot expect to achieve the maximum results of this material if you are not committed to achieving these results. In order to achieve your ultimate goals and dreams in life, you must have a starting point and take action.

I know this sounds a little harsh, but as your coach I must and will hold you accountable for your actions and your failure to take action. My ultimate goal is to assist you in achieving your Why in life. At times I am like a drill instructor whose purpose is to turn green recruits into full metal jackets. I am very serious about helping you to Find Your Why and Fly. I hope you are serious enough to "Just Do It."

What is Commitment?

Commitment is a serious, even sacred, pledge to do or be something. It is hammer-hard determination to achieve. Like a full-metal jacket bullet, it is so focused on the goal that it blows right through the obstacles and distractions.

Commitment takes us beyond comfort zones and personal indulgences. The Oxford English Dictionary actually says that commitment is "an engagement or obligation that restricts freedom of action."

Think about that. Being committed to a goal means we have to give up some of our freedom. For example, if I'm committed to investing twenty percent of my income, I may have to give up the freedom to buy all the latest electronic toys. If I'm going to lose forty pounds in the next six months, I may be forced to give up my freedom to have a glass of milk and cookies before I go to bed.

Are you committed – REALLY COMMITTED – to your own success? Is that commitment strong enough to finish reading this book? Be honest. How many books have you bought and not read? How many books have you cracked open, read a few pages and then stuck on the shelf?

Now, I'm going to challenge you to read this book...every lesson, every word. Upon completion of reading each lesson of this book, write a summary of it in your learning journal. A learning journal doesn't have to be anything fancy. A basic notebook will do. It is critically important to write down what really hits you out of each lesson. I also refer to this as brain-spilling. Regularly and frequently summarizing each lesson is the best way to get life-changing truth off the page and into your heart and mind. By reading it, writing it down and reviewing it frequently, you internalize it. You take possession of it. You take ownership of the truth that will set you free!

Remember, I said earlier that we must all read or listen to something at least seven times before we truly grasp the concepts of the material. You should also write in your journal each time you re-read it. You will see that each time you read the book, your journal will reflect different thoughts and ideas that will dramatically change your life if you commit to them. Even the seventh time!

What will Commitment Do in My Life?

I believe that commitment is the key to achieving the level of success that your Certificate of Life guarantees that you will achieve. Not only is commitment a full metal jacket, it's also life's cement.

Strong foundations are not made of sand. A foundation must be strong enough to hold everything stable and steady during a storm or earthquake. That's why foundations are made of cement. Your commitment to achieve your dreams is your life's cement.

When you have a cement commitment behind your dreams, nothing will stop you. You will stand tall through the storms of life and create a safe atmosphere for yourself and your family. When everyone else says it's impossible and you will fail, your personal commitment provides another voice. That voice says, "You will persevere and win!"

How to Maintain Your Commitment

Over time, even cement will crack and break. Think about strolling down a sidewalk and looking down to see the weeds growing between the cracks. Your life's foundation can also crack and allow weeds to grow. These weeds are often the naysayers and the critics that don't believe in you or your right to achieve success.

Repairs are essential to keeping your commitment foundation strong. If you don't create and maintain a strong cement foundation of commitment in your life, then you will allow the negative weeds to get between you and your dreams.

How do you maintain your commitment? First, you must read and re-read the right books and write in your journal every time that you read them. Books like Napolean Hill's "Think and Grow Rich" or "The Richest Man in Babylon", or the one you're holding now are great assets to your success library.

Second, spend time with successful, positive, encouraging people. Some people just radiate success, confidence and commitment. Hanging out with them will help to maintain your own foundation of commitment. When you spend time with negative, doubtful, mistrusting people, you will damage your foundation.

Jim Rohn, one of my mentors, says that we should regularly ask ourselves, "Who am I with? What are they doing to me? Is that good?" I agree. You've got to commit to yourself that you will not hang out with and be a victim of dream stealers. No one but YOU owns the title deed to your life. Out of respect for yourself, commit to spending time with people that are victors in life. Be committed to walking in victory!

Third, forget the mistakes and negative defaults of the past. You're free! Kick your chicken and leave the shackles of your past behind.

You must be determined to develop your commitment long term, because success is not easy.   Failure is guaranteed if you are not committed to your success. Daily commitment to the achievement of your Why will push you through the trials of life. It's like physical exercise; it must be done daily!

An essential part of maintaining your commitment is to stay away from cynics and dream stealers. Join others that have made the decision to walk in victory! Don't let negative people determine your level of success.

If you read the right books, journal your thoughts, spend time with positive and successful people and leave your past mistakes behind, you will find that your foundation of commitment will harden just like cement and become stronger each day.

> No one but YOU owns the title deed to your life. Out of respect for yourself, commit to spending time with people that are victors in life.

Think about it for a second. When cement is first poured, it is not hard. Sometimes people will actually write their name in it while it's wet.

Once the cement is hardened, it remains that way forever with proper maintenance. In the same way, once your commitment hardens in your mind and heart, it will remain that way. It's up to you to keep the naysayers, your negative past and other discouraging factors from defacing your commitment before it is hardened into a strong foundation in your heart and mind.

I'm a New Yorker, but I like the song of the wide-open West, "Home on the Range." I like it mainly because of one line, "where never is heard a discouraging word." Think about that. Do you care enough about your own success to live in an environment that contains no discouragement? Are you so committed to your future that you will surround yourself with people, books, CDs and movies that encourage rather than discourage you?

Never forget that the power of your commitment is one of the greatest factors in your life. Your commitment to success or your commitment to your cycle of failure will determine whether or not you achieve your life long dream.

Let's try to understand this. The word "power" means the authority to take control over. You need to take control and authority over your lack of commitment in the past and recommit to your achievement of your goals and dreams.

If you are a success maniac like me, then commit yourself to your own future. This type of commitment gives you both the right and the power to achieve your ultimate Why in life. Behind every Champion's achievement of their Why is a strong and solid commitment. When you're on track and have commitment as hard as cement, your foundation doesn't move around. Yes, you're hard-headed. You're solid as a rock! You are going for it! You're making decisions like a committed Champion!

That's where it all starts to come together and before you know it, your life takes off like a space shuttle and people standing around suddenly jump back, look startled and say, "Whoa! What happened? What's going on with you?" What they're seeing is the blast-off of your success rocket, the manifestation of your commitment.

That's why commitment is one of the most important keys to success. Remember, your commitment is the foundation, and it's your decisions that will determine whether or not your foundation will crack in the midst of life's storms.

Now, I want you to write out your commitment. Write down what you are committed to doing with the rest of your life and what obstacles you are committed to avoiding.

_____

_____

_____

_____

_____

_____

_____

_____

_____

_____

_____

_____

_____

_____

_____

_____

_____

_____

_____

_____

_____

_____

_____

_____

_____

_____

_____

_____

_____

Lesson 3
The Habit of Giving

People often ask me things like, "John, what is the main habit of multi-million dollar entrepreneurs, life-changers and dream achievers?" There is no question at all in my mind that the number one habit of all of those people is giving.

Before we move on to discuss the ultimate success factor, which is the manifestation and development of your Why in life, I want to discuss this one habit that will have a great impact on your level of success. It's the habit of giving.

As you begin developing your Why and reading other Champion Why Cards in this book, you will see that many people like you want to help others by giving away a percentage of their success. When I read some of my student's Why Cards, I see things like "I want to donate $10,000.00 dollars to my favorite charity" or "I want to tithe $50,000.00 to my church."

I believe that we are all born with the desire to bless others. We all want to give back. We have an inbred need to make other people's lives better. I believe that we are created in God's image, and he is very generous. Therefore, it's only reasonable to believe that we as human beings are generous. It's only the negative scripts in our society like "always look out for number one" that turn us from generous to selfish.

I've learned that the best exercise in the world is to reach down and lift someone up. The sad thing is that we lose sight of helping others when we are so focused on ourselves.

You really do want to give financial blessings to others; you want to give your time; you want to invest your energy in noble causes. Based on your need as a human being to give to others, you must make the decision to include the habit of giving time, money and energy in your Why.

The Mystery of Sowing and Reaping

I know that you may not be accustomed to giving freely especially when you have never had that much to give. It's uncomfortable at first, but the giving habit makes you a stronger person. I truly believe that you will sow what you reap. Most people are familiar with that principle or at least that phrase, but think about what it means.

If you sow wheat in a field, the crop that pushes through the soil to be harvested is wheat. It is not and will never be corn. If you plant an apple seed, the green shoot that springs from the ground will not become a pecan tree.

> We cannot sow a selfish attitude and expect to reap abundance and generosity. It just doesn't work like that. If we make giving a habit, then life has a way of giving back to us.

We cannot sow a selfish attitude and expect to reap abundance and generosity. It just doesn't work like that. If we make giving a habit, then life has a way of giving back to us. All successful people even non-religious ones know and practice that exact concept. Let me say it again. If we make giving a habit, then life has a way of giving back to us. That knowledge is one of the greatest commonalities of successful people.

Trust me. If you make the habit of giving a main priority in your life, then you will be blessed beyond all of your goals and dreams that you've ever imagined of achieving. Now, let's get you started on your habit of giving by saying the following out loud: "I am a daily giver. I will commit to giving daily to others."

How to Get Started in the Habit of Giving

Obviously, you don't start out by distributing one hundred dollar bills as you walk down the street. You can give in many ways. Here are a few ways you can start to cultivate this new habit:

- Donate your time to your favorite organization or a friend in need.
- Offer your wisdom to person that may be starting a new life for himself/herself.
- Smile and say hello to someone that looks like they really need something positive to happen to them.
- Take some of your old clothes that you never wear to the Salvation Army.

- Cook a hot meal for an elderly shut-in.

- Repair an automobile for someone that can't afford the repairs.

I would say that the first rule of giving is very simple - give what you have. If you don't have wealth, you may not be able to give money, but you can still be a giver. You can still cultivate the habit of giving.

First, give whatever you have been blessed with or whatever talent you have. You have to sow these seeds today in order to design your future. You design and predict your future by planting seeds in the lives of others. If you plant seeds of hope in others, then you will reap a bountiful harvest (a successful future).

Of course, there's a flip side to that. If you are selfish and only think of getting what you want out of life, then you will reap what you sow – selfishness. Your failure to plant seeds in the lives of others will result in nothing but dried up soil not to mention a very lonely and unfulfilled life.

There's nothing better than the feeling you have after you have blessed the life of another person. For instance, my wife and I decided five years ago not to give Christmas gifts to each other and even asked our family/friends not to give us Christmas gifts. Instead, we take the money that everyone would have spent on those gifts and provide a great Christmas for families in need. Christmas is our favorite time of the year not because of what we receive, but because of what we give away and the joy that our giving brings to others.

Anyone Can Give

Some of you will say, "You know what John? I just can't give right now because I have nothing to give." You're wrong. A smile is a gift. A handshake or an embrace is a gift. Being there with a shoulder to cry on is a gift. Being accountable to your business partner is a gift. Being a daily giver and planting seeds in the lives of others will change the face of your future.

Always remember, seasons come and seasons go, but seed time and harvest will not cease no matter what we do. Think of it this way. If you plant a seed in the summer, then you will reap its fruits in the fall. If you fail to plant a seed in the summer, then in the fall you will have no harvest. The great Jim Rohn says, "Everyone must be good at sowing in the spring or will be begging in the fall."

The habit of giving is like insurance for the achievement of your ultimate Why in life. For example, if you have a car

> Don't be misled. Remember that you can't ignore God and get away with it. You will always reap what you sow!"
> - *Galatians 6:7*

accident then your insurance guarantees that your damages will be covered based on the amount that you provided in your policy. It's the same with giving. Your habit of giving determines your level of success in your future; it is based on what you have given away.

Many people think that they will wait until they are a multi-millionaire to give. That is not the way to start. The sad reality is that if you can't bring yourself to give now, then you sure won't make yourself give when you are financially secure and wealthy. Remember, giving is an attitude; it is not based on the amount of money in your bank account. It's a heart issue. That's why I say that anyone can give.

You Can Only Keep What You Give Away

I heard an incredible true story that I want to pass on to you. A young couple had not been married very long when the husband began to feel a strong sense that they should give away their household possessions. Furniture. Appliances. Even wedding gifts. Everything! After a few days, he reluctantly shared his feelings with his young wife only to discover that she had a very strong sense of the same thing. She had been struggling with how to tell him.

Confident that God was directing them, they began the process of giving everything away. Within a few days, everything was gone. The husband recalls, "Even the original painting that my grandmother had painted, a family heirloom, was given away." Although somewhat perplexed as they slept on the floor amidst nothing, they felt peace and assurance that they had done the right thing.

A few weeks later as they were driving home, they saw smoke rising from the landscape. As they drove closer to their neighborhood, they realized the smoke was billowing up from their property. Their house was consumed by flames and burned to the ground.

A few nights later after they had settled into temporary housing, car lights appeared in their driveway. A friend walked to the front door carrying the gift that this young couple had presented to him a few weeks earlier. During the next few days, a steady stream of cars came to their home returning nearly every item they had given away.

Years later, the husband said a very profound thing, "We learned at any early age that you can only keep what you give away. Today, we once again treasure my grandmother's painting. It only hangs in our home because we once gave it away."

That is so true. If we hoard our treasures, then they shrivel and disappear. If we give them away, then they return to us. Learn to create the daily habit of giving, and at the conclusion of your day ask yourself, "What did I do today? What seed did I plant today in order to predict my future?"

> If we hoard our treasures, then they shrivel and disappear. If we give them away, then they return to us.

Remember, whatsoever you sow you shall reap.

I want to ask you a bold and provocative question: "If you sow nothing, then how can you have the audacity to expect something in return?" That would be like not planting any seeds in your field, but expecting a corn harvest. First comes the seed you plant and then comes your harvest. Never forget that.

Plant something everyday! Do not end your day without giving something away whether it's a smile, a big tip to a waitress, a dollar to a homeless man, a huge tithe to your church, etc. Give someone the opportunity to have their life changed by you being a better person.

Understand this: you are a uniquely privileged individual, because you are holding this book in your hand. Millions have lived and died without ever finding the secrets to success. That means you are 99.9% ahead of everyone who has ever lived. Be grateful for all that has flowed to you and from that gratitude bless others. Allow them to reap some of your blessings by developing the habit of giving.

If you read about the truly wealthy entrepreneurs like John D. Rockefeller and Mary Kay Ash, you will see that in the end those Champions were giving away more than they earned, which means they started the process of giving early in their careers. When the famous Pastor W. A. Criswell of First Baptist Church of Dallas retired, he gave the church a check that was more than all the salary checks he had ever received. I challenge you to model your life after those great people by developing the habit of giving today.

Write down how you will begin the habit of giving. What will you give away on a daily basis? How will you impact the lives of others?

_____

_____

_____

_____

_____

_____

_____

_____

_____

_____

Lesson 4
It is All About the "WHY"

Yes, you read it right. It is all about the WHY! A strong enough Why will pull you through every situation and will make you a true conqueror and victor in every occasion. It will lift you far above the average. It makes you go where others stop. It pulls you though the swamps of life when others get stuck, lost or drowned.

I can almost hear what many readers are thinking..."Is this it? How can these words bring all the lofty promises you just made? How can it be that simple? This sounds too simple to be true."

> Goals are great, but a "Why" separates a goal-setter from a goal-achiever and a person that truly changes people's lives!

I agree that it's simple, but it's not too simple to be true. In fact, I've learned that most of life's secrets of success are simple. Too often a false intellectualism makes things too complicated to ever succeed. Yes, it's simply all about the Why.

The Miracle Inside

You're Why is your biggest, most significant, result-creating force in life! Goals are great, but a Why separates a goal-setter from a goal-achiever and a person that truly changes people's lives. Another way of looking at your Why in life is to think of it as your ultimate reason or purpose for living.

Your Why makes all the difference in your life. It separates you from the crowd. A strong Why will not only make you get up in the morning, but it will make you happy, passionate and want to live your life to the fullest!

My goal is for you to "Find Your Why." Discover that driving force inside of you and feed it with the right words, the right people, the right books, the right motivation and the right inspirational messages. If you do that, then the force – your Why – will emerge and drive you to success. Do you realize that you have a miracle inside you? We just have to extract it and enable you to fly. As I say, you've got to Find Your WHY and Fly!

Let me tell you my story. At the age of twenty-four, I was working seven days a week, more than twelve hours a day, in my family business, an art gallery. My grandfather, who I truly loved and adored, gave me two of the most powerful values that I still possess today - honesty and hard work.

I graduated as an elite business student from an accredited college, but it got me absolutely nowhere. I respect education, but most of the time education only teaches you about a certain subject. It doesn't train you to achieve success.

That is part of what makes my teachings and this book so different. My goal is to train people and motivate them to become successful no matter their level of education, where they came from or any other factor that society uses to determine success. EVERYONE can do it!

As you know, I was a stutterer. But, worse than that, I was labeled a stutterer. People would tell me, "John, just stay with your family. That's all you're gonna do. You'll work for your family. Don't worry about becoming successful, forget your college degree. You can't even say your name! Who do you think you are? How can you get a regular job? How can you take your college degree and go out and change the world?" I was labeled by society and destined to fail if I listened to them.

If you have been labeled, I want you to tear that label off of yourself right now! A label is a lie. Labels box people into groups. As I wrote in Lesson One, we are not a group. We are individuals. When people called Helen Keller deaf and dumb, they were labeling her as part of a group of handicapped people. As a strong individual with a miracle inside, she blew through that group label like a bullet through a bed sheet. That so-called handicapped lady is one of the most successful people in history.

> "What lies behind us and what lies ahead of us are small matters compared to what lies within us."
> - Oliver Wendell Holmes

No one deserves to be labeled no matter the challenges that they face in life. The miracle inside is larger than the label, and inside you are seeds of greatness. The famous and wise Oliver Wendell Holmes said, "What lies behind us and what lies ahead of us are small matters compared to what lies within us."

Learn to Fail Forward

At the age of twenty-four, my life changed when I was introduced to a person that told me, "You can do whatever you want to do in life." I was so excited yet I was scared to death! I couldn't even say my name without stuttering. Could I really do it? How did I meet this person that finally gave me the belief in myself that I had desperately been seeking? I simply answered an ad that said "Make $10,000 a month, wear tailor-made clothes, and drive Mercedes Benz." I still have the actual phone that I dialed to respond to that ad, because that ad changed my life forever.

I answered the ad and went to an event. The event was on March 15, 1990 at 7:30pm. That night, I was introduced to a business. Most people will be introduced to something that could help them achieve their Why, but they won't do it. Why? They won't step out in faith or take a risk. In order to succeed in life, you must fail forward. That's right...fail forward. This means to face your obstacles head on and keep going toward your goal no matter if you succeed or fail. Again, be a full metal jacket. Blow right through obstacles and even the appearance of failure. Every time you take a risk or you fail forward, you will be a little bit closer to achieving your Why in life!

Don't ever forget this: Every failure is a stepping stone to success, which in turn becomes a very long and lovely stone walkway into the castle of your dreams.

Getting Beyond Security

I was introduced to a vehicle that enabled my Why to finally come alive. I listened to a woman speak about a business and a vehicle – Network Marketing. I'll never forget her words.

She said, "If you work hard, if you work smart, if you follow a system, you will achieve success."

She also said that I could achieve these three magical words - time, freedom and wealth. That's when I saw the possibility that even I could do what I wanted to do, when I wanted to do it and with whom I wanted to do it with. Within seven years of hearing her speak those words of power into my life, I created a very successful business and semi-retired to South Florida.

Yes! I grabbed those words that created the possibility that I could succeed like a drowning man grabbing a life preserver. I said to myself, "I want to empower people. I want to help people realize that they can do whatever they want to do in life." For the first time in my life, I was able to move beyond the comfort zone of security.

I realized that my security of working behind the scenes at the art gallery had allowed my stuttering to control me and my life. Security will make you complacent. It will control you and ultimately destroy you. If you're secure right now in your job, you could be in the process of demolishing your future success.

Let me ask you a question, if you didn't have to go out and earn money to pay your bills, what would you do? That's right; if every bill was paid and you had enough money in the bank for the rest of your life, what would you be doing? Take a second and write down your answer. Now, that is your Why!

> If every bill was paid and you had enough money in the bank for the rest of your life, what would you be doing? Take a second and write down your answer. That is your Why!

I will come back to that later, but let me tell you what happened when I went home that night from the event. I arrived home to my parent's house about 11:30pm, and I just started crying. Why? Because I found a way out! I found the actual vehicle that would allow me to achieve my dreams. I could build a business, set myself free and be able to go out and speak to people. I could tell others that it is possible to achieve success, and it is okay to have dreams. That's the night my life and my world changed.

Then, I was introduced to personal development through the classic book, "Think and Grow Rich" by Napoleon Hill. If you don't have that book, then invest in yourself and go buy it. Personal development and the industry of Network Marketing opened my eyes to opportunities that I never knew existed or were possible for even me to achieve.

I woke up the next morning and was on my way to the gym at 5:30am. As I was driving to my health club I thought to myself, "I truly don't understand yet how I'm going to do this. I don't know this business. I don't know the system. I don't know anything", but what I did know was that someone told me I could do it and I was willing to listen to that person.

I was willing to be become success-driven and listen to people that could and would help me become successful and achieve my Why. To do that meant leaving the comfortable and complacent nest of security. You will never fly, and you will never become a success maniac if you remain in the nest.

Facing Your Fear

About a week into my new business, I attended a seminar. I knew that I would have to stand up and say my name. There I was, labeled a stutterer, sitting at that seminar, listening to people introduce themselves one by one. It was almost my turn, and I walked out of the room. Why? Because I knew I couldn't say my name. I went in the bathroom and sat on the floor and cried. I had convinced myself that there was no way that I could say my name.

What did I do? I remembered my Why, faced my fear and went back inside. I still remember standing up, my knees shaking, heart pounding and sweat coming off me like a waterfall. My eyebrows were even twitching! You know when you're so nervous you can't catch your breath? That's where I was that night. I said, "My name is Ja-Ja-Ja-Ja-Ja-Ja-Ja." I couldn't say my name so I just sat back down in my seat in shame, but that moment was a breakthrough. I vowed that would never happen to me again! As I drove home that day, I said to myself, "No matter what I do, I will never quit!" Guess What? I NEVER DID!

If you have fear in your life, you have to face it, attack it, demolish it and pulverize it. I had to do it, and you have to do it. We all have to face our fear in order to achieve our Why.

> I still remember standing up, my knees shaking, heart pounding and sweat coming off me like a waterfall. My eyebrows were even twitching! You know when you're so nervous you can't catch your breath? That's where I was that night.

Champion, where are you in life? It doesn't matter how far you are from where you want to be in your life. You can produce miracles! I believe you can do it. Do you believe you can do it? Just like me and millions of others, you too can achieve the impossible!

Expect miracles each day. I do. Why not you? YOU CAN DO what you would do if every bill was paid and you had enough money in the bank to last for the rest of your life. You can find out that it is all about the Why.

Many of you reading this book have created a bond with me simply by reading this material. From now on, I want to be your coach, your mastermind team member and your accountability partner. Are you ready? Let's go!

Lesson 5
Finding Your Why in Life

I told you earlier that I teach my students to take action steps. I have discovered the power of actually standing up, speaking words out loud and writing down specific exercises. There's no thinking about it or overanalyzing each step. Just do it!

Now, we are at the point for you to make one of the most important decisions in life. So, stand up and say this out loud:

"Today, I have started my journey to find my Why in life. Life will test me at certain times. But, NO MATTER WHAT, I will complete my journey. At this very moment, I decide that I will NEVER quit this journey!"

How does that feel? I know it might have felt a little awkward, but most people likely felt some type of relief. Remember, what you just shouted out loud is a promise to yourself! Now seal this promise by writing the exact same words that you just said on these lines and shout it out loud

seven times – DO IT NOW!

_____

_____

_____

_____

_____

_____

What Does Your "Why" Mean?

Before we start discovering your Why and unleashing your

untapped powers and genius, let's take a second to focus on the

Why. What is a Why? What does it mean? Your Why can be

defined as your reason or your purpose. It is the reason or

purpose that you take up space on this planet.

One of the definitions of "Why" in The Oxford Dictionary

is "for what reason or purpose?" The same dictionary defines the word "reason" as a cause, explanation, or justification. Furthermore, the Oxford Dictionary gives one definition of "purpose" as the reason for which something is done or something exists. Another word that is frequently used when describing a Why is "mission." The Oxford Dictionary refers to the word "mission" as an assignment.

Whatever term you personally like is up to you. This bit of research will give you some strong references about your Why and how to unleash the Champion inside of you. What other words would you use to define your Why?

_____

_____

_____

_____

_____

_____

_____

_____

How to Find Your "Why"

Over the years, I've learned that often a person's Why is buried down deep inside underneath feelings of doubt and insecurity that have built up like barnacles on a bottom of a ship. The good news is that we – *YOU* – can and will extract your Why. By harnessing courage, you can confidently go to the next level in your life. As I told you, my goal is to assist you with finding your Why no matter how deep it's hidden inside of you and no matter how much negativity we have to scrape off the top of it.

In order to help you find your Why, let me share some more of my story as well as some other electrifying testimonials. The power of this story will inspire you and help you discover your Why in life. It will also ignite a burning desire within your guts to start digging and polishing your Why.

You will begin to see, understand, discover and feel that your Why is the #1 factor that determines all of your successes and failures for the rest of your life. That's right. Your Why is the ultimate success factor. As your coach, I am committed to give you all that I have in order to motivate and inspire you to achieve your Why. In everyday life, your mind might choose your profession, your hobbies, or the way you spend your leisure time. But, your heart always chooses your Why.

I'm asking you stop rushing your life for a few moments and make room in your heart for that spark to ignite. Let your heart out of its cage. Release your heart to dream about an unimaginable future. Don't you owe that to yourself? Is the rest of your life important enough to make this investment in yourself? You need to write down your thoughts and expand on them. You've got to be open to receive.

> Let your heart out of its cage. Release your heart to dream about an unimaginable future. Don't you owe that to yourself? Is the rest of your life important enough to make this investment in yourself?

Even as a stutterer, I knew my Why was to change people's lives. When I went out to that seminar, I didn't see just a business. I saw a vehicle that would allow me to attain my Why. I saw a vehicle, a means of transportation, that would empower me to set goals and achieve financial freedom so I could fulfill my Why.

Let me ask you, "Have you thought about what vehicle will drive you towards achieving of your Why?" Do you know what it is? Some of you may know, and some of you may still be searching. That's fine. Just begin to daydream about it. Daydreaming is one the best and most dynamic part of a true champion's day. Write down your vehicle or vehicles that will assist you in achieving your Why in life.

_____

_____

_____

_____

_____

_____

_____

Now ask yourself, "What is my Why?" What is your passion, your purpose, your ultimate goal in life, etc.? What would you do if you had all the money and time that you ever needed? Let your heart soar and write down your thoughts on the lines below. If you run out of space, grab another piece of paper and keep on writing. Let your future flow through your pen. Do not edit or correct it yet, just keep on writing. Let it flow from your heart. Letting the emotion really flow will create massive movement. Go for it!

_____

_____

_____

_____

_____

_____

_____

_____

_____

_____

_____

_____

_____

_____

_____

_____

_____

_____

_____

_____

_____

_____

_____

_____

_____

Your Why must be bigger than who you are right now. Remember, your Why is your ultimate dream, goal and desire in life. If you are having some difficulty discovering or writing your Why, then here's one of my student's Why Cards as an example.

My Why is...

"I am dealing with all the challenges of building my business today, because my WHY is to spend more time with my family, provide for my children's education, and have the finances needed to take regular family vacations and be a mentor to my kids. I am donating/tithing a percentage of my earnings to my church or favorite organization. I am making a difference today as a Profit Producing, Fear Demolishing, Record Breaking, Action Taking, Eye Opening, Mind Blowing, Fired Up and Laser Focused Millionaire Champion."

That's a very powerful Why Card, but the first day that I sat with this individual she didn't say all that. I had her write down the three magical words - My Why is. She took those three words home and let her heart do the rest, and that is how she ultimately wrote the magnificent Why that you just read. After she wrote her Why and internalized it, her business grew threefold.

Now we have expanded on developing a Why, let's dig a little deeper in your own Why in life. Let's crystallize your initial thoughts a little more by rewriting your Why. That's right, do it again and write from your heart.

My Why is...

_____

_____

_____

_____

_____

_____

_____

_____

_____

_____

_____

_____

_____

_____

_____

_____

_____

_____

_____

_____

Once again, your Why must be bigger than who you are right now. In fact, I will let you in on a little secret. You

> A genuine Why should scare you a little bit! The sheer possibilities of it should blow your socks off.

should think so big that it actually scares you into success. That's right. A genuine Why should scare you a little bit! The sheer possibilities of it should blow your socks off. I remember the title of an old novel, "Sometimes a Great Notion." A true Why captures the possibilities of what happens when "sometimes a great notion" seizes your heart. When it seizes your heart, it takes over. It will drive you! That's part of the secret of Rick Warren's phenomenally successful book, "The Purpose-Driven Life." Your purpose *(your Why)* will drive you!

A true Why will ignite that spark in your heart and fuel your dreams. Your Why will change your daily actions and drive you to places that you've never seen or considered before. Your Why will pull you through the ditches and dirt of life. It will set you apart from the crowd. It will give you that little bit of extra that makes you happy, passionate, proud and prosperous in all areas in your life.

I know there is a WHY in you! It might be covered by a layer of unproductive programming, and you might not feel worthy of achieving anything greater than what you are right now. That's OK. Don't worry about it. Things will begin to change simply, because you have ignited a powerful spark inside of your heart. You did it by simply writing out your Why!

It's like a seed that has fallen into the soil. It will take on a life of its own. You don't have to keep digging it up to see if it's growing. All you need to do is give it some time. This moment, later today or tomorrow, find a place where you feel comfortable and open up this book again. Start reading it from the very first page. Take your time to ponder, think and write. Take your time to feel the spark. Finally, write down the three magic words, "My Why is." Write it all out again. Write it as though it's the first time. No, it's not redundant. It's an action step on your road to success. It's recommended by your coach, mastermind team member, and accountability partner - ME! I promise you that when you follow these exact steps, your spark will ignite and you will be on fire for your life and your Why.

For years, and probably decades, you've been beat up by negative words in every part of your life. What words? Well, any of these sound familiar?

"You can't do it!"

"Who do you think you are?"

"You're nothing special!"

"Don't you know where you came from?"

"Who are you trying to kid?"

"Remember when you failed at..."

Erase those words from your memory and vocabulary. I am telling you: YOU CAN DO IT! Whatever lingers deep inside your heart, YOU CAN DO IT! Remember, I couldn't speak fluently for the first twenty-four years of my life. I was told to stop trying, because I couldn't even talk. I was doubted by almost everyone in my life based on the label that was stuck on my forehead by society. Does this sound familiar to you?

I couldn't speak fluently, but my Why was big enough and strong enough to pull me through the impossible. Every day I stood there by the Hudson River, screaming letter after letter until I completed the entire alphabet. My miracle happened one letter at a time. I did it and so can you!

Your birth certificate *(Certificate of Life)* gives you the right to go out and achieve all your goals, dreams and desires in life. Remember, we all start on equal ground with our birth certificate, but it is up to you to make your life different from the average, normal person that just settles for what they are handed in life or for whatever security that have found that protects them from facing their fears. Find your Why and fly!

Lesson 6
Unleashing Your Why in Life

By now, I'm sure you're well on the way to finding or perhaps you have already found that spark inside your heart. That spark is what ignites that roaring fire of desire deep inside of you. I salute you! You're doing something that most people never achieve. You're discovering your ultimate Why in life. Writing your Why is a process, and you can rewrite it as many times as you need in the beginning phase. Every great accomplishment starts with one step towards its achievement.

The Incredible Power of a 3x5 Card

There is one more secret that I have to tell you before we continue our discussion on the Why. You are likely wondering "how" you will achieve your Why. I believe that 95% of your success will be a direct result of the power behind your Why and only 5% will come from how you will actually accomplish it. In other words, don't worry so much about the how, just keep focusing on the Why at this point. My own experience is that if your Why is strong enough, then you will never have to worry about the how. Strangely enough, the how will present itself. I've seen it happen many times.

Now, let's talk about the power of your Why. The way for you to unleash the explosive power locked inside of your Why is simple. Grab a 3x5 index card. I'll say that once again. Grab a 3x5 index card. This is a million dollar tool, but it is so simple that most people won't do it! You could have expensive software that will allow you to create a fancy, multi-colored, seven-dimension,

> Start internalizing your "Why" in your mind, your heart and your spirit. It will change your life forever, and you will never go back to that point you were at before you found your "Why".

micro-chip implanted Why card. You could have every fancy tech gadget under the sun, but this little 3x5 index card will change your life.   It will massively change your life!

At the top of the index card write "My Why Card" in big letters. Then, write your personal Why statement on this card beginning with "My Why is." After you've done that, you must commit to reading it over and over and over again! The power of the "Why Card" lies in its mobility. You can take it everywhere you go, and you will never lose focus on the achievement of your Why.

With every challenge or obstacle in life that you face, simply face it head on and READ YOUR WHY CARD. Start internalizing your Why in your mind, your heart and your spirit. It will change your life forever, and you will never go back to that point you were at before you found your Why.

The 1st Seven Minutes of Each Day

Listen up...this is your coach speaking. One of the most important daily action steps is that you read your Why Card for the first seven minutes of your day. It is of the highest importance that you spend the first seven minutes of every day reading your Why card. That's right. When you wake up in the morning, the first thing that you MUST do is read your Why Card. It's called the "Why Rollover." Rollover, grab your Why card and read it!

Imagine reading your Why Card the first seven minutes of your day instead of picking your cell phone up, checking your email, clicking on TV and watching everything bad that is happening in the world. Isn't your Why more important to you than those things? Start internalizing your Why. Start meditating on it for seven minutes early in the morning when you get up. This meditation period will set your day on fire! It will add a snap to your step and a smile to your face, because you know your Why. You know why you do what you do every single day and that you will ultimately achieve your Why in life!

Write this down and *say it out loud*:

"I have decided that I will read my Why Card every morning for the first seven minutes of my day. I will

internalize my Why and feel my heart grow full of joy,

excitement, determination, and creativity every day because I

know my Why!"

_____

_____

_____

_____

_____

_____

_____

The Last Thing Every Night

What's the next step? Let me give you another million

dollar tip that will catapult your belief in your Why. Here it is.

Read your Why Card before going to bed and meditate on it for

a few moments. Go over the day and ask yourself, "What did I

do today that will assist me in the achievement of my Why?"

Then ask yourself, "What can I do tomorrow to improve my daily championship action steps that will ultimately lead to the achievement of my Why?"

Write all these things down in your personal Why journal. Just like the 3x5 index card, use a simple notebook for your Why journal. A Why journal is a tool that you can keep on your night stand or near your bed. Every night, jot your answers to those two questions.

1. "What did I do today that will assist me in the achievement of my Why?"

2. "What can I do tomorrow to improve my daily championship action steps that will ultimately lead to the achievement of my Why?"

These Champion habits will pulverize old, unproductive behaviors. These habits will increase your success pace drastically! I know many of you are saying to yourself, "But, I don't have time to read the Why Card in the morning and at night."

Let me ask you a heart-wrenching question, "Are you committed to achieving your Why in life?" If so, then you will soon realize that the amount time you invest reading your Why Card every morning and every night will determine when and if you achieve your Why in life.

The Purpose of Problems

The number of obstacles that you face in life will lay the foundation for massive growth. One of

> The ultimate success is always hidden by problems. In solving them, you acquire skills that you need to be a leader.

the most important principles to understand as you build your future is that problems have a purpose. A wise man once said, "The doorway to success is camouflaged by problems." That's why there are challenges, obstacles and hurdles between you and your Why.

That's the reason I often say and even wrote in the introduction to this book that my stuttering disability turned into a precious gift in my life. It became the driving force behind me creating the most powerful success key - "Find Your Why." Success is always hidden by challenges and problems. In solving them, you acquire skills that you need to be a leader.

Just as the butterfly must struggle to shed its cocoon, we all have to struggle to climb out of failure and into success. In fighting its way out of the cocoon, the butterfly develops muscles that it will need to fly. I once heard a man describe trying to help a butterfly get free of its cocoon. He took a knife and cut the cocoon away. The butterfly came out, but then died right before his eyes! That butterfly needed – and we all need – the struggle to achieve.

The great Russian novelist Aleksandr Solzhenitsyn once said, "Even biology teaches us that habitual well-being is not favorable to life." We all need to struggle our way into success. Striving to succeed will always be part of achieving your Why.

When we don't have struggles or obstacles to overcome, we become complacent, lazy and passive.

My coaching student that wrote the Why statement that you read earlier certainly understands that. That's the reason that she began her Why by saying, "The reason why I am dealing with all the challenges. . . " She didn't flinch at the possibility of obstacles. She embraced them. Just settle it in your mind that you will have challenges, you will have obstacles and you will have hurdles—no question about it!

That same champion student also uses the words, "I actually see..." This is a critically important key in the process of overcoming the problems. You must SEE yourself successful, and you must SEE yourself achieving your Why. That's why many successful sports trainers make their students visualize the golf ball rolling into the cup, the basketball swooshing the net, the arrow hitting the core of the target, etc. If you see it, you can do it. If you can't see yourself (visualize) achieving your Why, then your belief in your Why is not strong enough.

The discovery of your Why is a great milestone in your life. You will change, and you will improve yourself. Your interests will change, and you will expand. You will enjoy life even more than you already do. In order for this to happen, you must invest in yourself, face the problems and see yourself achieving your Why.

Lesson 7
The Growing Why

Your Why is a burning desire. It is the driving force that makes you achieve your ultimate goals. As your life progresses and your horizons expand, your Why will also naturally progress. Here's an important principle: Your Why expands as you grow.

With your Why growing and expanding, it is very likely you will notice more changes in your life. All of the sudden, you change your habits and you are more interested in investing more time in your personal development. Personal development is the key to advancing yourself mentally, physically and socially in order to achieve your Why.

The Power of Other People

As your Why expands and becomes more developed, you will find yourself growing past some old friends and your current lifestyle. Just visualize adding a drop of water to a glass everyday. Soon the glass will overflow, and you will need a bigger glass. It's the same with your Why. You will out grow the everyday normalcy. Your Why will start spilling over into every part of your life, and you will start to reach for bigger and better things.

It may be painful or difficult, but creating change in your life always provokes change in your friends. It often takes courage and resolve to make those changes especially when it means that you must leave behind people that you have known all of your life. Many times, those same people just fall away when they see the new you. However it happens, change will always bring new friends and lose some old ones.

One of the principles in Napoleon Hill's "Think and Grow Rich" is to let great people shape your life. That principle will always carry us away from people who are not great and will only keep us from achieving our Why. It is very likely that you will decide to just stop associating with certain people in your life. Some people have the unfortunate power to disconnect us from achieving our Why; therefore, we must make the decision to stop allowing those people to steal our dreams.

An accomplished and successful musician once said, "Critics are only remembered for what they failed to understand." Don't allow the critics in your life to kill your dream. Too many people have lost their dreams, because they have surrendered to the challenges that life threw at them. Those same challenges are often thrown by people that don't understand and simply can't hear the music in their own heart.

Many champions that disconnect themselves from the critics find themselves entering into a lonely, isolation zone. This is normal. It's just part of the "friend exchange" that goes with your new life. You must be determined to surround yourself with other Champions that believe in you and want you to succeed. These people are your mastermind team.

Your mastermind team should consist of people that will walk with you on your path to success. They are people that will encourage you as you face challenges that threaten the ultimate achievement of your Why. Do you have a Mastermind Team? Let's see.

Write down the top five people that you associate with on a daily basis. Please be truthful.

1.

2.

3.

4.

5.

Now, cross off those people that are hindering and holding back your success. These are the critics that simply can't understand your music *(your Why)*. They refuse to believe that you can and will do better things with your life. Don't be surprised if you are left with only one or zero people out of those five. I've seen so many people give up on their dreams and the achievement of their Why, because they simply didn't have a Mastermind Team to support them.

The Lifestyle Freedom Club

It's very frustrating for me to see Champions fail because of their everyday associations with naysayers. That's why I along with my team decided to take action and create the Lifestyle Freedom Club. This is the #1 fastest growing success and motivation club in the world full of other Champions just like you.   I believe this club is a MUST for dream builders. Why? As I said before, it is very hard to achieve your Why by yourself. You need a support system, and someone that believes in you. Start building your mastermind team today by visiting

<u>www.LifestyleFreedomClub.com</u>. Find out how you can build your own mastermind team of Champions!

By changing your actions in life, you will change your results. By changing your results, you will notice that the quality of your life improves. This all happens, because you took the time and effort to find and ultimately achieve your Why in life.

Write down five action steps that you are committed to taking as you relentlessly pursue your Why.

_____

_____

_____

_____

_____

_____

_____

_____

Lesson 8
Infect Others With Success!

Do you remember the principle of sowing and reaping? This is an important key to success. You can soar to unparalleled heights in your life, and part of what carries you there is the power of sowing the right kind of seed. Learn to share, influence and improve the lives of others. Basically, if you want to radically change your life, make sure that you commit yourself to assisting others and leading by example.

As I said before, there is no better exercise than reaching down and lifting someone up. We all have a need to help others and to give back some of what we've been given. When you read the Why statements of Champions, you will see that golden thread running through everything they envision for a successful future.

For example, when I first went out to the bookstore to pick up "Think and Grow Rich", I proudly showed it to everyone around me. I told them that if Napoleon Hill's son could be cured of deafness, then I would be a fluent speaker. Although this seemed impossible *(always remember inside the word impossible is possible)*, I was excited to share it with my friends and family. Sharing makes you bigger and makes you accountable to yourself and others.

Don't be afraid to share your feelings and don't be afraid of one or two negative reactions. Most people think negative and will respond to your dream of achieving your Why with negativity. You must continue to tell your friends and family about your Why and your longing to better yourself and your life.

Tell them that you feel that they can also achieve miracles in life. Tell them they need to start by finding their Why and then actively pursuing it. From that point, follow-up with them about their progress and share your progress with them. This will show them how much you care about them, but it will also assist you in the ultimate achievement of your Why. You are sowing seeds into the lives of others, and you will reap a bountiful harvest.

Lead by example. After you share your Why with others, they will watch you a little closer. They will notice that you are

> Tell them they need to start by finding their Why and then actively pursuing it.

changing. They will see that you enjoy life more and that you are achieving massive results. This will inspire them to ask you, "What has happened with you?" This is simply positive reinforcement that will assist you to face the challenges that life throws at you and achieve your Why. I want to see success spread like a prairie fire across the world. My personal dream is to see millions connect with their own personal Why and achieve success beyond their wildest dreams.

Now, create a plan of action that includes you sharing your Why with others and describe how your Why will impact their lives. Go ahead, take action now!

_____

_____

_____

Lesson 9
More Magic behind the Why

I want to share a real-life example with you. One of my students catapulted his life to new levels, because he discovered and applied the true power behind the Why. Now, I am going to breakdown his Why so you can feel and find the power behind it.

First, he wrote *"MY WHY IS . . . I am a home-based entrepreneur, because I am an optimistic maverick at heart. While I am a team player, I feel passionate about being responsible for my own growth and happiness rather than dealing with a coarse and cutting senior manager controlling my destiny. I do not care to be dependent on some company's time schedule, budget, or benefit plan."*

This is great stuff! He is announcing who he is, what he's passionate about and what he will no longer tolerate. He doesn't want to deal with certain influences and limitations anymore. You can tell that he despises those things and knows that they are stopping him from achieving his Why.

He goes on to say, *"Every day, I will listen to 50 minutes of coaching CDs/DVDs and read personal development and leadership books . . . 50 minutes a day to become more efficient and more effective."*

This man is so focused! He is making a deliberate choice to only eat and digest the right mental foods. He's saying that what he listens to is important. If he listens to junk, he'll become junk. If he listens to successful coaches, then he will become successful.

Then he writes, *"My vision for 2012 is to be healthy, free and committed to helping create 1,000 millionaires. My vision is to help 1,000 freedom-oriented people become lifestyle freedom coaches and millionaires. Yes! I will help create 1,000 millionaires in my lifetime."*

Very powerful and focused. Once again, he's speaking his Why forward. It's more than feelings or vague desires. He is speaking activity. He is speaking Why words. His Why is bigger than who he is! Remember, your Why must be bigger than who you are. It must change the person who you are. If your Why is not so big that it changes who you are, it's not big enough. I'll repeat that again. If your Why is not so big that it changes who you are, then it's not big enough!

Now, I want you to break down your Why like I did with the Why above. You must know and understand your Why inside and out. Your Why is the foundation of your success in life and must be rock solid.

Break down your Why. Use a separate sheet of paper if you need it.

_____

_____

_____

_____

_____

_____

_____

_____

_____

_____

_____

_____

_____

_____

_____

_____

_____

_____

_____

_____

_____

_____

_____

_____

_____

_____

_____

_____

_____

_____

_____

_____

_____

_____

_____

_____

_____

_____

There are three major obstacles that will hinder the achievement of your Why if you don't take action. As we progress through these obstacles, I'm going to bring you back to times that life threw these same three major obstacles at me to distract me from achieving my Why life.

What are the Obstacles?

These obstacles and problems will actually serve a purpose in achieving your Why. What are they? The first obstacle that will hinder the achievement of your Why is the group of toxic people around you. These people will tell you things like, "Are you crazy?" "Who do you think you are?" "You're not going to build a business!" "You're not going to earn that kind of money!" "You're not going become financially free!"

That's why I call them toxic people. They will poison your success journey. Do not let negativity just ooze onto your doorstep! Here's what I've learned. Love your friends that do not support you moving to the next level in life, but make a decision today to move on from them. Of course you love them, but you have to love yourself enough to leave them and stop them from stealing your dreams.

Remember this: leaving them is also an act of love. Go find your Why, achieve your dreams and then come back later to share your success with them. In other words, when you have built a strong foundation and developed strength by believing in yourself, you can reach out to them. This is a simple technique called love them, leave them and show them.

Have you ever noticed that when flight attendants prepare the passengers for the flight that they talk specifically about the oxygen mask? They say, "In the event of a sudden cabin depressurization, oxygen masks will drop down. Please secure your own mask before helping others." That's not selfish! If you don't guarantee your own oxygen flow, then you won't have the strength or consciousness to help anyone else. In the same sense, go work on your own dream. When you've discovered your Why in life, you can go back and sow seeds of greatness in the lives of those same people that tried to hold you back.

The 2nd obstacle that will hinder the achievement of your Why is your past. Visualize your past as chains shackled to your ankles. Let's talk about those chains. Everyone has experienced failure. Everyone has made mistakes. Everyone has done stupid things. The past can only hold power over your future if you let it! That's right. Your past will haunt you for the rest of your life if you let it.

It will drag you back to the place that you were before you found your Why. It will also prevent you from moving forward towards the achievement of your Why. You have to ask yourself an honest question and more importantly answer it. Are you letting the chains of your past hold you down? If so, I suggest that you look down, take the chains, throw them away and never look down again.

Harriet Tubman is known for abolishing slavery in the United States and was once quoted as saying, "I freed thousands of slaves and could have freed thousands more if they only knew that they were slaves." This great quote applies to life in general. Many times, we simply don't know what is holding us back; therefore, we are unable to take the action needed to create massive success in our lives. You must be aware of what is preventing you from gaining freedom in all areas of your life before you can ultimately achieve your Why.

The 3rd obstacle that will hinder the achievement of your Why is giving up. It is easy to give up and say to yourself, "This is not going to work! I can't do it! I quit!" Many years ago, I remember opening the door to the Rye Town Hilton. I walked up the stairs to the meeting room and saw a sign-in table. Immediately, the little inner voice said, "Ha ha! You have to say your name! Go back to the art gallery loser! What are you doing out here? Just go home, eat, watch TV, go to bed, wake up and do it all over again the next day just like you've done for the last twenty-four years."

But I stepped out in faith! I didn't know back then what faith was or how to take a risk. I simply had no clue, but I didn't give up on my dream. As I progressed towards the table, I saw a sign-in sheet. I looked down and the man at the table said "What is your name?" I grabbed a blue tag and I wrote my name down. I flipped it around, and he read it. He said, "Oh, hi John!" I said "Hi!" Why? I was too afraid to say my own name, because I knew that I would stutter.

I am now an international motivational speaker, accomplished author, mentor to millionaires and a strategic business coach. How is this possible for a stuttering fool? I knew my Why and I did not quit! I say that with full conviction and confidence, because I know that you can do it too. Right now, I want you to write down the following words and internalize them - Failure and quitting are NOT options!

_____

_____

_____

_____

In order to achieve your Why, you must have those words

instilled in your spirit and believe that you will succeed no

matter what.

Lesson 10
View from the Mountain

When we discover new and life-altering truths, we are like pioneers standing on a mountain ridge looking at a new beginning. In the cool, crisp morning air, we can see forever. Then, our gaze slowly and finally settles on a beautiful valley. The vivid colors of the grass and lakes and the framing horizons of sky and mountain peaks are just breathtaking. In that golden moment, our heart says, "Yes. That's it! That's where I want to spend the rest of my life." We can hardly wait to get down there and go to work building our future. Our heart almost explodes as we imagine breaking the sod, planting crops, building a house and joining with other like-minded people in creating a new community. We are seized by "Sometimes a Great Notion."

We finally arrive in that valley and begin to carve out that new life. At first, it's romantic and exciting, but after a while reality sets in. We discover that it's too hot in the summer and too cold in the winter. Mosquitoes, crickets and rattlesnakes can make life difficult. When we initially saw the gorgeous and lush green meadow from the mountain top, we didn't realize that much of the meadow was filled with weeds. At that point, the faint-hearted will become discouraged and begin gazing at the next mountain range. They end up forsaking the valley in pursuit of another dream. Too many remain wanderers in life, drifters away from the dream and always preoccupied by new mountain ridges.

For example, some people are like that regarding their own marriage. They begin in great excitement, romance and passion. But when they get into the hard work and heavy lifting of building a life with another person, they get discouraged and start looking for someone else.

Refresh Your Vision!

I've learned that when discouragement sets in, it's best to go back to the mountain top where you stood the first time your eyes fell on that valley. Refresh your vision! Remind yourself of the great possibilities that you once saw. For instance, go back in your mind to when you first met your husband or wife. I'll talk to the men for a second, but ladies this also applies to you. What was it that you saw in her? Remember the way that she held her head and smiled as she listened to you talk. Remember how she laughed when you told a joke. Remember how your eyes filled with tears when you saw her coming down the aisle of the church on your wedding day.

> . . . when discouragement sets in, it's best to go back to the mountain top from which you saw the first time your eyes fell on that valley. Refresh your vision! Remind yourself of the great possibilities that you once saw.

Sometimes, we just have to go back and revisit the view and refresh the vision that we had from the mountain. That applies to our Why as well as to our spouse. No matter what, your Why is still there as radiant and full of possibilities as ever. You just have to refresh your vision of what you saw the first time that you ever imagined it or wrote out your Why Card.

In this last lesson, I want to take you back to the mountain and refresh your vision. I recommend that you re-read this lesson *(return to the mountain)* once a week until it's inscribed in your heart and mind.

Let's take a few minutes to climb back up to the peak from which you first saw the possibilities of a new life. Here are some of the things you saw:

Find Your Why and Fly!

I want to break this down word by word so you can get a renewed vision for it.

- **Find**

    You have to FIND it. Your Why will not seek you out. It will not hunt you down and wrap itself around your life. You have to dig, search, excavate and often get frustrated or even angry as you work to FIND it. Olympians spend years practicing and training for the Olympics prior to ever attending the actual events.

They are laser-focused on winning a gold medal. You have to display the same kind of tenacious, relentless and patient focus on FINDING your why.

- **Your**

  We're working on YOUR Why not mine and not anyone else's. You are responsible for it not me, not your mother, not your spouse, not your boss. You own it! If your Why doesn't challenge you to discover and fulfill your ultimate purpose in life, then YOU are the one that has to figure it out. You and only you. It's YOUR Why!

- **Why**

  This is the core, the center of your life. It is the driving force. It's the "north star" of why you even take up space on the planet. Your Why is your reason for living. It's your most compelling purpose. If it doesn't scare you, it's too small. If it doesn't change you, it's an insufficient Why.

- **And**

  The simple word "and" is a very important conjunction. According to Webster's New World Dictionary "and" means next or thereupon or in addition to. In other words, Finding Your Why leads to something else. "And" also establishes the order. In this case, you have to Find Your Why and only THEN can you Fly! If you try to fly first, then you will end up flat on your face because you haven't learned to use your wings.

- **Fly**

  Jim Rohn talks about living where you want to live, wearing what you want to wear and driving what you want to drive. In other words, a vital part of life is getting to taste the sweet fruit of success. Finding your Why leads to flying. Of course, you can't do this part first. The fruit, the result and the outcome of finding your Why is the ability to fly beyond all of your hopes and dreams. It's your ability to finally understand what success feels like.

Here are some other things you saw from the mountain ridge:

Reclaim Your Birthright

Never forget that the most important day of your life is your birthday. That's why the day is special. That's why you *(and those who love you)* celebrate it. It's more than just a cultural thing. We have a sense down deep in our heart that the day is significant.

Why? First off, because of the way sperm unites with the egg, we are all a miracle, literally a one in a million success! At birth, we all start out the same. We're on the same planet, we're subject to the same natural laws, and we all begin our lives in the womb as a miracle of success.

That's also why our birth certificate is so important. It is a legal document that gives you the right to grow up and become a Champion. That piece of paper is your Certificate of Life. Unlike working for a college degree, you automatically earn your Certificate of Life when you exit the womb. No questions asked . . . you are destined for success.

Refuse to be a Victim

Our society carries a relentless temptation to blame someone else. Victimization is the ethic of our times. It has a way of becoming our work ethic *(the boss or the company are the reason we don't succeed)*, our marriage ethic *(our spouse keeps us from becoming who we were meant to be)* and our life ethic *(because my mother or father or 3rd grade teacher damaged me with their insults, I will never be a whole person)*.

When we break the cycle of blame, we take responsibility for our own life. It is only when we decide to stop blaming others that we begin to succeed.

(Re)Program Your Computer

Our life's default program is one of discouragement, temptation, fear, anger and doubt. It projects discouraging, dangerous and defeating messages. This default program comes mostly from television, newspapers, music, movies, billboards and real live people. All of us walk through a daily bombardment of programmed words that are highly toxic.

Here's the process by which the default programming is installed on our internal computer. What comes in our ears, enters into our heart and then comes out our mouth. *Ears > Heart > Mouth*. Even Jesus said we are defiled by what comes *out* of our mouth. Just further proving that this is not a new concept.

We have to re-program our internal computer. We have to deliberately choose the software that will make it run clean, smooth and fast. That software is a combination of the words that we read and the words that we hear. These words form the attitudes, thoughts and expectations of our life. Therefore, we must be careful what we watch and read. Words are some of the most powerful things in life. They are seeds. When these seeds fall into the soil of our lives, they take on a life of their own. The seeds start to develop roots, take over the field and create a massive crop. That's why we have to be vigilant even militant to only sow the right kind of seeds.

I rarely watch TV. Why? Because it's like inviting a negative, lying, cynical and flirtatious person to live in my house. Why would I do that? Why would I invite someone I didn't trust or even like to live in my house? I'm always amazed when I hear parents talk about having to monitor the TV for their kids. Would they invite a dangerous, crazy person to live in their house and then feel the need to be present every time he talked to their kids? NO! Not only would you NOT invite someone like that to live in your house, but you would get a restraining order to keep them far away from your house and your kids.

The reason I'm writing so much about TV is that in our society television is probably the biggest source of programming that goes into our internal computer.

Forget the Past

All of us have made mistakes, committed sins, disappointed our family and friends, and even injured other people. Those things can be haunting, but all that we can do is to try to make things right with people and move on.

Most of us have also had great successes in our past, and sometimes the successes are as restricting as the failures. When we have an image of something we accomplished, that image often has a way of blinding us from seeing the brand-new possibilities that may be different and better than what we've already attained.

For some reason, we have trouble escaping our past failures and successes. As long as we are a prisoner to the past, we can never fully embrace the new future that awaits us.

That's why the Apostle Paul, one of the greatest figures in world history, said "... one thing I do: forgetting what lies behind and reaching forward to what lies ahead, I press on toward the goal for the prize of the upward call..." - Philippians 3:13-14.

Our past has no hold on us. It can only hurt or be an obstacle if we allow that in our mind. That's the lesson of "kicking the chicken." Let me refresh your memory. When farmers take chickens to the market, they will often tie their ankles and lay them in the bed of their truck for the ride to the

> ". . . one thing I do: forgetting what lies behind and reaching forward to what lies ahead, I press on toward the goal for the prize of the upward call. . ."
> – Philippians 3:13-14

sale barn. This prevents them from flying out of the truck.

When they arrive at the sale barn, he will take them out of the truck, place them on the ground, and then cut the cords, releasing them to get up. But, the chickens won't get up! They think they're still bound at their ankles, so they just lay there.

The farmer has to actually kick them to stir them to flutter and get up. We sometimes must "kick the chicken" in ourselves in order to get out of our obsession with our imprisonment to our past. So, "kick the chicken" in yourself. Your ankles are free! Get up and walk around. Celebrate your freedom.

Discover the Power of Commitment

Commitment is the foundation for building your life. It is the bedrock of achieving your ultimate Why in life. Commitment is that hammer-hard, burn-the-boats, full-speed-ahead determination to do, to be and to achieve something. Nothing, absolutely nothing will stop a person of genuine commitment.

One of the main reasons that Champions have commitment is to just get through the clutter, the confusion and the noise in our society. We are saturated with lights, colors and voices. It's so easy to just flop down and watch TV or go hang out at the local pub. To really focus on achieving massive results requires a very serious commitment to our own future. Do you have that kind of commitment?

For example, do you make appointments with yourself? Do you make them with your own spouse and children? A genuine depth of commitment will cause you to take your own life and your family seriously. We schedule time for meetings with our business associates, beauticians, bankers and others that are far less important to us than our own future and our family members. Perhaps our priorities need to be remodeled.

Every champion, every success maniac, should commit to regularly scheduling time with a good book or a conversation with his or her spouse or quality time with his or her children. It is also important to schedule time with other Champions. Let them infect you with their success and winning attitude.

Build a Habit of Giving Generously

If you knew that all healthy people had one thing in common, wouldn't you want to know that one health secret?

Well, if you want to be magnificently successful, you need to know the one victory secret that Champions have in common. That one thing is the habit of generous giving.

Giving is an attitude. It finds real and deep joy in blessing other people. To give generously is to discover a secret fountain in the heart and when you give your life away, it always returns to you in fuller, deeper, richer measure than it was when you gave it away. Sowing and reaping are principles of the universe. Whatever and however you sow is the same measure by which you will reap. Take that to the bank!

Embrace the Miracle!

Every person in this world is unique. There are no two people Exactly alike, and every person is a miracle. Just the fact that you were born means that you have already beat the odds.

We are all caught in a war. Part of the war is the chorus of voices that try to devalue your uniqueness and steal your dream. Those voices even try to make us part of a group. A major part of embracing and celebrating the miracle is to reject the label. You are not a group. Always remember that you are YOU!

Keep Moving Past the Obstacles

The three main obstacles standing between you and success are:

1. Toxic people

2. Your past

3. Giving up

Set your face toward your future and move right on past those obstacles. Do not be distracted by anything or anyone. It's YOUR life! Don't stop or take a detour. Remain focused on the goal and keep moving.

The Bible tells the story of Jesus healing a paralyzed man. What Jesus said is very instructive for us, "Rise, take up your bed, and walk." I think he may have told him to pick up his bed in order to remove the temptation of falling back into bed! Once you pick up your bed, it's easier to remain focused on walking. As long as the bed beckons, we're always tempted to quit.

Face Your Fear

Fear is no stranger to me. I've told you my story of stuttering, but you have a story of fear too. In fact, everyone reading this book knows fear. Most people assume that they have some special fear. That's simply not true. Your fear may be slightly different than mine, but fear is universal. Everyone has it, and everyone has to choose how to deal with it.

If you are going to achieve greatness and be a champion, then you first have to face, attack, demolish and pulverize fear. I had to do it. You have to do it. We all have to face our fear in order to achieve our Why. Don't let fear intimidate you. Remember that everyone that ever lived had to deal with fear. You can and will do it!

"Why" is More Important than "How"

Having a strong and focused *WHY* is vastly more important than knowing *HOW* you're going to achieve it. The Why will give birth to the How. If you focus on the How, then you'll never have a large enough Why.

Sometimes I think the news media has turned us into "how addicts." You've heard it all. . . *"How* will you do that, Mr.

> Having a strong and focused "north star" of purpose is more important than knowing "how" you're going to achieve that purpose. The "why" will give birth to the "how."

President?" *"How* can we ever solve a global crisis like AIDS?" *"Give us the details on how* you can balance the budget, Governor."

Focusing on how introduces fear and doubt. If you work at thinking through the How, then you leave too much room for fear and despairing doubt to seep into your mind. Again, Nike's ad line is helpful: "Just do it." The How will show up at the proper time!

OK, I guess it's about time to go on down the mountain and back out to building your dream. Remember, you need to come back here about once a week.

Reading this book has been an exciting journey, hasn't it? The fact that you completed this book and have found – or are in the process of finding – your Why in life proves to me that you are destined for greatness.

I won't say that your journey to the full development and enjoyment of living your Why is going to be easy, but you hold a great key to success in this book. I don't say that because of my ego. I say it, because the truths in these pages are time-tested and proven to be effective. They worked for me, and they have worked for literally thousands of successful people.

You have been given an iron-clad, blueprint that will guide you through the basics that you need to "Find Your Why and Fly!" You are a Champion! If you've not already done it, take time to Find Your Why.

Always remember, my fellow Champions, that when the crowd of "they" say there's no sense in going further and that everything has already been explored, don't believe it! Don't settle for mediocrity. Just keep listening for the sound of that little voice within that continues to tell you that it is possible. It still calls out just as strong and just as clear as it did to Thomas Edison, Andrew Carnegie, Napoleon Hill, George Washington Carver, Helen Keller, and thousands of other Champions throughout history.

That something hidden down deep inside is your Why. It waits. Go and search for it. It is waiting for only you! When you find it, write and tell me about it. Send me a copy of your Why Card. I want to hear *YOUR* story.

Oh, and one final thing. Remember to join the Lifestyle Freedom Club. We're all familiar with Clubs. People have clubs for real estate, movies, books, knitting, sports, etc., but how many of you have ever belonged to or even heard of a Club devoted strictly to building motivation for success and provides resources to assist you on your journey? Imagine it - a Club that only exists to help you find the right motivation, provides life-changing resources and gives you the ability to hang out with mastermind team members that will support your dream and encourage you toward the fulfillment of your Why. I believe this Club is a MUST for dream builders. Start learning how to live the lifestyle that you've only dreamed about today by visiting www.LifestyleFreedomClub.com.

Why Cards of Champions Just Like You

"My Why is to live an extraordinary and passionate life filled with love, laughter and gratitude. I wake up every morning feeling inspired and excited about the miracles ahead. I change people's lives every day. I inspire millions of girls and women to share their fabulousness with the world, to embrace their unique gifts, to make them feel that the impossible is possible. I help people discover and achieve their dreams and provide valuable tools and resources for them to achieve success whatever that means to them. I am excited and committed to learning and growing every day. I am financially free and do what I want when I want and with whom I want.

I love my life and I soak in every single moment of every day that God blesses me with. I speak positive, energetic, life changing words that inspire others to dream big, love life, make a difference and smile. I bought my parents a gorgeous home and send them on vacations regularly. I have a husband who loves and adores me. We love each other unconditionally and passionately. We challenge each other to be the best we can be, we respect each other, we laugh all the time, never take each other for granted and cherish all of the amazing memories we create. We donate our time to charities and we tithe and give back to our church and community. We raise our children to be thankful for life and always go after their dreams. We encourage their creativity and feel blessed knowing that they will make a difference in the world. I am my word and live with integrity. I am an amazing mother, wife, daughter and friend and am completely loyal to those I share my life with. I am living my purpose and thank God every day!" - *Kate Volman, Florida*

"I am diligently building my business today by sharing the gift of hope, health, and opportunity by doing all I can to become all I can and giving all the glory to God. I am changing the lives of a million people worldwide through personally enrolling one thousand associates that share my vision for total financial freedom and want to make a difference. As I do this, I am a loving and caring husband and father. I am enjoying an abundant lifestyle and am building a lasting inheritance for my children and my grandchildren. I tithe to my church, donate to Acts One Eight and MannaRelief Ministries. I am a blessing to others. Today, I am making a difference." - *Michael Peters, United Kingdom*

"My Why is to change people's lives and provide them with great value. I will always speak God's truth and wisdom. I trust God to guide my path in obtaining an abundant life. My gallery and my art is the current vehicle to provide me with abundant income to take care of my Mom, create financial independence for me, and give much to my charities of choice.

Right now, I am enjoying living my ever expanding WHY. My WHY is the PROCESS. Listening, learning and changing is a BLAST! I am financially free and doing what I want to do, when I want to do it, and with whom I want to do it with. I am no longer a diamond the rough. I am a precisely cut diamond in the process of being highly polished to more valuable than the HOPE diamond....PRICELESS!

Day by Day my income is increasing, my physical health Is improving, I am looking and feeling younger. My mental clarity and concentration are consistently improving. I am known worldwide as the highly enthusiastic, happy, healthy, helpful, hugging ENCOURAGER who listens with a laser focused heart and mind. My Christ centered life is creating daily, abundant miracles." – *Bev Ervin, Florida*

"My Why is to be a wildly successful, unstoppable, inspirational, influential, invincible Presidential Leader of my money making, cash flowing, tithing companies. I will promote, protect, and preserve the branding of the heart of Roger Farkash, T W Design and TrainWorx. I will nurture the Farkash Four Family Legacy. I am ready! I am 100% Laser focused and today and forever more! I will joyously and enthusiastically share the Love of the Holy Ghost that dwells deep inside my heart and soul. I love you God, I need you God, I trust you God, I thank you God. May you flow through me each 86,400 seconds in this day!" – *Dorcie Farkash, Texas*

"As a life-affirming, action-taking, fear-demolishing, fired-up champion, I am living into MY potential DAILY! I am consistently presented with the opportunity to impact others in positive ways through opening relationships. Borne out in a lifelong purpose of providing for others, my devotion to serve is anchored in the bedrock of family legacy, childhood dreams, years of focused education and *my* long standing desire to make a difference in the lives of others.

Moment by moment, I endeavor to connect with others, including those receptive to a perhaps yet unrecognized need for lifestyle changes. As a result, many people are discovering and acknowledging hidden dangers of popular lifestyle choices.

These individuals also strongly desire to globally impact multitudes of people in positive ways.

As I continue my positive, personal evolution, I am serving greater numbers of people by diversifying my services and am committed to tithing a higher percentage of my own monetary rewards. Further, I volunteer my time and efforts to medical missions through Mercy Ships, a global organization that has operated hospital ships in developing nations for more than thirty years. With them, I bring hope and healing to the forgotten poor worldwide, and serve ALL without regard to race, gender, or religion.

In developing, refining, and following *my* life plan I continue to tithe and volunteer, as well as travel at will, for both leisure and visionary work. I continue to live comfortably and will do so throughout my own *long* life. I am associating with countless others of like mind and have found and am nurturing a wonderfully healthy and committed relationship with my lifelong partner, in shared vision. I am living in immense gratitude daily." - *Pam Phillips, Florida*

"I am a giving, loving, sensitive woman who helps individuals and groups fulfill their dreams, as I fulfill mine. I am a mentor to millions worldwide, sharing my experiences and giving encouragement. This is ordained by God – I have just finally come to the understanding that I don't have to do anything more than be a willing voice that follows direction. What a refreshing and joyful realization! No more stress about ANYTHING!

As the journey continues, I am not only mentoring millions worldwide and introducing them to the power and freedom found in faith; I am also finally able to RECEIVE. My income far surpasses what I need to live on a monthly basis, which gives me so much income that I can fill the needs of those around me, as the Lord leads. I am meeting incredible people, creating new friendships, and loving them unconditionally. I am also very relaxed and social with my kids, family and friends – free of the fear of what others may think!

I have been able to achieve Lifestyle Freedom and have a four bedroom, 3 bath home with a large office and meeting area in the rear - and a beautiful pool and spa with tropical foliage and rock waterfalls. I am completely debt free, including my home, car, and businesses. I have ample funds in reserve to leave an incredible legacy to my two daughters. I am loving the travel time as I meet new people all over the world!

My health is exactly where it needs to be and I am exercising regularly, loving every minute of it. I am also playing the piano and singing to increase my relaxation and make the most of my devotional and study time. I have also learned to relax and play; no longer the workaholic. I am holding seminars, workshops, and networking events to help others build their businesses and grow in their personal relationships. This includes working with churches and other organizations to increase membership and reach the needs of children, youth and adults.

I am continually staying connected with like-minded people; staying true to my convictions; updating and changing my "WHY" as it grows and evolves. And most of all, giving thanks to God that I made the CHOICE to Find My WHY!" - *Leslie Mendenhall, Florida*

"I believe in myself one million percent. I am completely extinguishing fear out of my life, living a bulletproof life against fear, and living a life full of enthusiasm. I am as fearless as a kid, full of faith, living a breathtaking life full of laughter. I wake up every day of my life with pure joy, and talking, walking, breathing, exercising, building with confidence. I am laughing like a champion, I have the best laugh in the world. I am paying all the bills at our home, my mom will not have to pay a dime on bills, and giving my mom all the money and love she needs to live very comfortably. She will have enough money to hire a personal driver, especially when it`s cold in Montreal. I am also giving a room to my grandmother, she will have all the latest proven, time-tested mobility aids that will assist her on living a more comfortable life.

I own a barn with three horses, and go through the training process of becoming an amateur jockey. I donate thirteen million dollars to my church and other ministries. I see myself being in a great, motivating, invigorating, very energetic, fired-up relationship with a beautiful phenomenal girlfriend that I share my dreams with. I am speaking all over the world, to empower human being to believe, dream and take action, show them how they can also fly by finding their why.

I own The Miracle Rev-Up Center, where kids can come play, grow and learn that they are record breaking champions I will give out free winter gear, food to struggling families, and go to shelters and give fresh food to families in need. I also give assistance to pregnant teenagers that feel alone and don`t know where to go. The Miracle Rev-Up foundation will create shockwaves around the world. The impossible is possible for me! I am the Prime Time Billionaire!" - *Doris Bakana, Canada*

"I am financially free and I am spending more time with my family. My family and granddaughter, Jewel, are the largest part of My WHY. I have formed a Trust for her and future grandchildren. We have a condo in South Florida area for the cold weather months. We also have our summer home in The Great Smoky Mountains of Eastern Tennessee.

We have a RoadTrek RV for traveling to South Florida, speaking events, and mission locations in this country. It is used to travel around the country recruiting professionals for our mission teams and Vision for the Americas, our nonprofit corporation for our mission efforts. The Americas refers to the United States, Canada, Mexico, Central American Countries, Caribbean Islands, and the South American Countries. We will provide eye care services throughout these areas utilizing mobile eye clinics and mobile glasses fabricating labs to reach the most deserving of the rural areas (small towns and villages). We have a team of committed volunteers serving the needs of these great people. We work with other professionals to provide medical, dental, nutrition, clothing and home construction for these most needy of the Americas. Our Roadtrek will also be used to travel and present our work throughout this country and the Americas to secure additional support financially, personnel, and supplies for our needs to serve the less fortunate.

I have prepared myself mentally, spiritually and financially for this great endeavor. I am a committed Servant of Our Lord, a great motivational speaker to secure the personnel and materials needed for our success. We also earn a large portion of our income from sharing my story at speaking engagements and through the sale of CDs, DVDs and my bestselling books. My second book is titled "It's Never Too Late to Have an Awesome Life."

Nita and I live on 25% or less of our earnings. The remainder of our earnings goes to the churches, ministers, missionaries in this country and abroad, Boys and Girls Clubs, Jovenes en Camino (Boys Home in Honduras) and needy individuals in this country and abroad that need our support. I will be able to say at the end of my life: My life had meaning and lives on through my contributions into the lives of others." - *Dr. Benny McDaniel, Tennessee*

It's Your Turn!

Now that you've read some Why Cards of Champions from every walk of life, it's your turn to write out your Why Card again. Don't be afraid to dream. It doesn't have to be perfect, and you should expect it to change as you grow. I would love to see a copy of your Why Card and know what you liked best about this book. Email me at John@ChampionsLiveFree.com.

MY WHY IS...

_____

_____

_____

_____

_____

_____

_____

_____

_____

_____

_____

_____

_____

_____

_____

_____

_____

_____

_____

_____

_____

_____

_____

_____

_____

_____

_____

_____

_____

_____

_____

_____

_____

_____

_____

_____

_____

_____

_____

_____

_____

_____

_____

_____

_____

_____

_____

_____

_____

_____

_____

_____

_____

_____

_____

_____

_____

_____

_____

_____

_____

_____

_____

_____

_____

_____

_____

_____

_____

_____

_____

_____

_____

_____

_____

_____

_____

_____

_____

_____